Creating with Podge
with

Welcome to the world of decoupage! Everything about this world will surprise you. The techniques are simple, the tools and materials are easy to find, and the results are fantastic. The biggest surprises, though, will come from your own imagination as you start seeing decoupage surfaces and project ideas everywhere. Have fun!

LEISURE ARTS, INC. • Little Rock, Arkansas

Decoupage Basics

Decoupage is an almost foolproof craft. All you need to start are some pretty papers and fabrics, scissors, basic foam brushes, and decoupage medium, such as Mod Podge®. Other tools you have on hand, such as a craft knife and blades, ruler, paper punches, and fabric scissors, make working with decoupage even easier. A brayer is useful for smoothing out wrinkles in paper, but you can also smooth wrinkles with clean fingertips or a dry brush. Stiff bristle stenciling brushes or scumbling brushes work well on fabric decoupage projects.

Scrapbooking papers of all varieties and gift-wrap paper are great to use for decoupage. Purchasing complementary color packs gives you a wide choice of pretty prints, and you don't have to worry about matching colors! Cardstock is only appropriate for absolutely flat surfaces. Decorative napkins and tissue papers are best used on dimensional projects; use stiffer papers on flat surfaces. Tightly woven cotton fabrics will work on both surfaces.

Decoupage medium goes on milky-looking and dries clear. It comes in matte, satin, and glossy finishes. Choose the finish you desire for your project. There are specialty decoupage mediums for fabric or outdoor use, and textured and glitter-finish mediums as well. Look in your local craft store for a selection of decoupage mediums.

Clear acrylic-sealer spray gives body to thin papers like tissue paper or decorative napkins; it's also great for final finishes over completely dry decoupage medium.

Here are a few helpful hints if you're new to decoupage.

- *Use the right pair of scissors.* Most scissors are meant to cut paper; fabric scissors are meant to cut *only* fabric. Don't ruin a good pair of fabric scissors cutting paper.

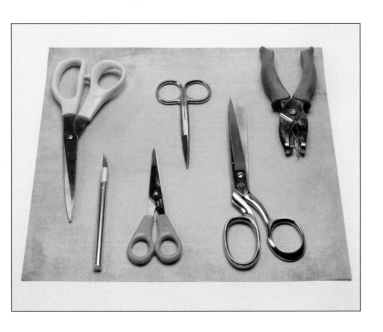

- *Clean fingertips are essential.* Use fingertips or a dry brush to smooth out wrinkles and bubbles. Your fingertips won't work well if they're coated with bits of dried decoupage medium!

- *You'll quickly learn to use the right amount of decoupage medium.* Too much medium will cause slippage, torn paper, and excessive drying times. Too little medium won't securely hold your paper.

- *Pay attention to the edges.* Make sure you have medium applied along the edges of your cut paper or fabric.

- *Let decoupage medium dry completely before you add additional coats.*

- *If it doesn't move, you can probably decoupage it!* Once you start, you'll see possibilities for adding a bit of decoupage to almost everything. Experiment and play!

Frosted Confetti Lamps

To begin the process:

1. Cut strips of tissue paper slightly wider than the size of each paper-punch shape.

2. Sandwich 4 to 6 strips of tissue between two pieces of copy paper. Punch out tissue shapes using a variety of punch sizes *(Fig.1)*.

Fig. 1

3. Apply a light coat of decoupage medium to a small area on the glass approximately the size of one of your larger tissue shapes. Place the shape on the glass and tap it lightly with a dry foam brush or clean finger, smoothing any wrinkles. Work gently or you may tear the shape! Adhere large shapes around the lamp, leaving spaces between them. Allow the paper to dry completely.

4. Apply smaller shapes to fill the areas between large shapes.

5. When all the shapes are dry, coat the tissue and glass with a light coat of decoupage medium.

DESIGNER TIP

Sandwiching delicate papers—tissue paper, napkins, and more—between copy paper prevents ragged edges on your punched shapes.

SHOPPING LIST

- ☐ coordinating tissue papers
- ☐ square and round paper punches
- ☐ copy paper
- ☐ matte-finish decoupage medium
- ☐ glass lamp

MAKE-IT-YOURS!

Dress up a plain lampshade with decoupage! Embellish a lampshade with as little as ¼ to ½ yard of fabric. See page 28 for directions on decoupaging with fabric motifs.

Summer Lights Candles

SHOPPING LIST

- ☐ candles
- ☐ scallop-edge tissue papers
- ☐ patterned fabrics
- ☐ clear acrylic-sealer spray
- ☐ copy paper
- ☐ gloss decoupage medium

To begin the process:

1. Wrap a strip of paper around a candle, mark the overlap, and cut the strip at the mark. This is the quick and easy way to make a template so you won't have to remeasure each tissue layer *(Fig. 1)*.

2. Decide on the height of the first layer of tissue and cut out a strip. Cut shorter strips for additional layers. Because tissue paper becomes somewhat transparent when you coat it with decoupage medium, always layer colors with the lightest color first and the darkest color last *(Fig. 2)*.

3. Apply medium over approximately ¼ of the candle, and then apply the first layer of tissue. Pat it in place with a foam brush or clean fingertips. Fold the paper back to apply medium to the next area of the candle, then ease the tissue onto the candle. Continue to work around the candle until it is covered. Allow it to completely dry.

4. Apply the shorter layers of tissue one at a time to the candle, allowing each layer to dry completely before applying the next.

5. Spray fabric with clear acrylic-sealer spray and allow it to dry. Cut out the desired pattern motifs and apply them to the candles with decoupage medium.

6. Paint the completed design with a coat of decoupage medium.

7. If desired, make a matching candle stand with additional tissue shapes. Review the directions in step 1 on page 21 for working on glass plates.

Fig. 2

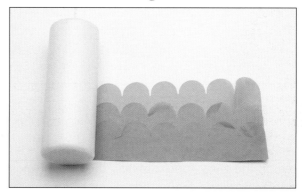

Fig. 1

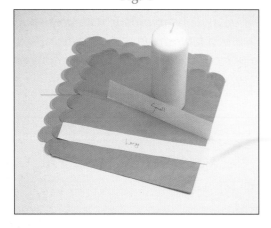

MAKE-IT-A-GIFT!

Candles, tissue papers, and scrapbook embellishments are all you need to create a quick gift during the holidays. Use a decoupage medium with glitter, such as Sparkle Mod Podge®, to add a sparkly, festive shine.

Letters Adorned!

SHOPPING LIST

- ☐ flat, wooden letter
- ☐ pencil
- ☐ copy paper
- ☐ coordinating scrapbook papers
- ☐ acrylic paint
- ☐ decorative paper tape or ribbon
- ☐ gloss or matte decoupage medium
- ☐ floral scrapbook embellishments
- ☐ low-melt glue gun and glue sticks

Fig. 2

To begin the process:

1. Place your wooden letter on a piece of copy paper. Draw around the letter to create a pattern for your shapes. Divide the outlined shape into large or small sections, as you prefer *(Fig. 1)*.

2. Use the paper pattern as a guide to cut the individual sections from patterned or solid-color scrapbook papers *(Fig. 2)*.

3. Paint the letter a color that complements your scrapbook papers. Pay close attention when painting the edges of the letter—it's easy to miss a space.

4. Brush a light coat of decoupage medium onto a small area of the letter shape. Apply medium to the back of one section and fit it in place. Smooth the paper with a dry brush or a clean finger. Continue applying shapes, fitting them together like puzzle pieces. Allow the letter to dry.

5. Add a strip of decorative paper tape where each shape meets the next. Wrap the cut ends around the back of the letter.

6. Apply one or two finish coats of decoupage medium to the letter. Allow each coat to dry before adding another coat. Glue floral embellishments to the letter with a glue gun.

MAKE-IT-YOURS!

There are many styles of oversized letters to decorate—plain wood, painted wood, and papier-maché. Papier-maché letters are fun to cover with decorative napkins or to collage with vintage

dress patterns. Always give papier-maché letter shapes a coat or two of white acrylic paint before you cover them with tissue or napkins.

Fig. 1

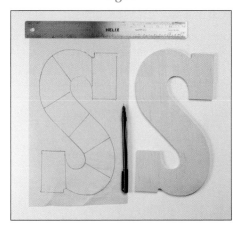

Old Blue's Portrait

SHOPPING LIST

- ☐ 4 canvas artist panels, 8" x 8"
- ☐ food coloring
- ☐ gloss or matte decoupage medium
- ☐ gloss or matte texturing medium such as Brushstroke Mod Podge®
- ☐ brayer (optional)
- ☐ recycled container (jar, plastic container, etc.)
- ☐ stiff bristle brush

To begin the process:

1. Scan a family photograph on your computer and crop the photo into a square format.

2. Import the scanned and cropped image into any photo-editing program. Remove the color profile to create a black-and-white photo. Apply an artistic filter to create a sketch-like image. Divide the image into four equal squares; cut and copy each square into a new document. Enlarge each image to 8" x 8". Print out the four documents *(Fig. 1)*.

3. Trim the printed images as needed. Adhere each image to a panel, smoothing out air bubbles and wrinkles with clean fingertips or a brayer. Allow the panels to dry. Give each panel a light coat of decoupage medium.

4. Pour some decoupage medium into a recycled container. Add food coloring a few drops at a time to the decoupage medium until you like the color. Paint a light coat of tinted medium to a desired area. Allow the area to dry before adding colors to other areas *(Fig. 2)*.

5. When all the panels are dry, use a stiff bristle brush to apply the texturing medium to each canvas panel in short bold "strokes." It's fine to brush on thicker than usual coats for this technique. Allow each panel to dry.

Fig. 1

Fig. 2

TIP

You can also take a photograph to your local copy store and have them enlarge and copy the photo for you. Buy your canvases before you go so you can determine the size of the copy you will need.

MAKE-IT-A-GIFT!

Make someone's significant birthday party a memorable occasion with a special portrait. Use a photo of the recipient as a toddler (cute) or teen (embarrassingly funny). You can also apply smaller copies to wooden ornaments for party favors for the guests to take home.

Personalized Scrapbook

SHOPPING LIST

- [ ] ½ yard each of two coordinating fabrics
- [ ] fabric scissors
- [ ] clear acrylic-sealer spray
- [ ] fabric-covered scrapbook
- [ ] fabric decoupage medium
- [ ] stiff bristle brush
- [ ] low-melt glue gun and glue sticks
- [ ] flat, faceted jewels or other embellishments

Fig. 2

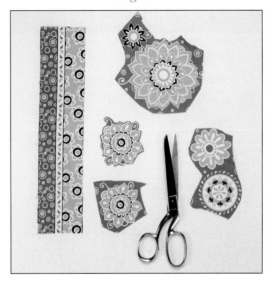

To begin the process:

1. Choose fabrics with bold motifs. This project uses two coordinating fabrics—one striped and one with floral designs *(Fig. 1)*.

2. Lay the fabric flat and spray the front of the fabric with clear acrylic-sealer spray. When dry, turn the fabric over and spray the back. The sealer will lessen the chance of the fabric raveling when you cut it.

3. Use fabric scissors to roughly cut out individual motifs on the fabrics, then detail cut the motifs. It isn't necessary to cut right up to the motif: leave a little bit of the background showing *(Fig. 2)*.

4. Arrange the motifs on the scrapbook; play with different arrangements until you like the result. Use a stiff bristle brush to apply the fabric decoupage medium fabric to the back of a motif. Pay attention to the edges as you apply the medium.

5. Place the motif in position on the cover, then use the brush to work medium into the fabric of the motif. Pay special attention to the edges to make sure they are well attached. Try not to go beyond the edge of each motif. Adhere the remaining motifs in the same way. When finished, let the motifs dry completely, and then give them an additional coat.

6. Add embellishments (rhinestones, buttons, etc.) to the scrapbook with a glue gun.

Fig. 1

MAKE-IT-A-GIFT!

Use this technique on other fabric-covered books. Look for a food-themed fabric to make a recipe book of family favorites for a bride. Make a new mother a baby's first-year book using children's prints or use exotic prints on a bound journal for a traveler's trip abroad.

Fanciful Flower Pots

SHOPPING LIST

- ☐ clay flower pot
- ☐ clear acrylic-sealer spray
- ☐ exterior acrylic paint
- ☐ fabric lace
- ☐ decoupage medium for outdoor use
- ☐ brush
- ☐ measuring tape
- ☐ painter's tap

To begin the process:

1. New clay pots work best for this project. If you're planning to place living plants in the pot, spray the interior with two coats of clear acrylic-sealer spray.

2. Use a measuring tape to determine the length of lace you'll need to wrap around the pot. Measure and cut the lace and set it aside (Fig. 1).

Fig. 1

3. Wrap some painter's tape below the rim to protect the unpainted surface of the pot. Paint the rim with two or three coats of paint (Fig. 2). When the rim is completely dry, mask off the rim and paint the bottom part of the pot.

4. Apply one row of lace at a time using decoupage medium. Allow each row to dry before adding another.

5. Apply two or more finish coats of decoupage medium to protect the lace.

Fig. 2

MAKE-IT-A-GIFT!

Tiny clay pots are quick and easy gifts for any holiday or event. Paint the pots inside and out with white paint. Apply tissue paper to the pots to reflect the reason—Easter, Christmas, Mother's Day, Halloween, or just because. Fill them with flowers, special treats, or tiny candles for special celebrations.

Elegant Storage Jars

To begin the process:

1. Use clip art or vintage images to create labels for decoupage. Import or scan images into a photo-editing program. Crop and size the images as needed for the jars you are using and place them in one document.

2. Cut a piece of white tissue paper slightly smaller than a piece of copy paper. Tape one end of the tissue to the copy paper. Test your printer to determine which side of the paper it prints on by marking an X on a blank piece of paper and printing it. This will tell you which side of the paper the images will print on. Now you know whether to place the tissue facing up or down in the printer. Print out your label images *(Fig. 1)*.

Fig. 1

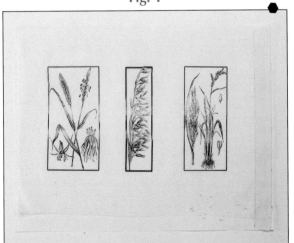

3. Cut out the labels and set them aside. If the glass jar you've purchased is colored, tint some decoupage medium to match with food coloring. Add just a few drops at a time until your medium is the color you desire *(Fig. 2)*.

Fig. 2

4. Apply a thin coat of medium approximately the size of your label to the jar. Place the label on the jar and gently smooth out any bubbles or wrinkles. Allow it to dry.

5. Give the label a finishing coat of decoupage medium.

MAKE-IT-YOURS!

Make a label for homemade gifts from your kitchen—dried soup mixes, party mix, or flavored liqueurs. Add raffia or ribbon to the container and you have a made-with-love gift.

martin
45 oak st.

Home, Sweet Home!

To begin the process:

1. Give the wood plaque—front and back—two or more coats of paint.

2. Use scrapbook paper to cover the flat area of the plaque. To copy any curved shapes, place a plain sheet of copy paper over the area. Run the side of a pencil point along the sharp edge to create a pattern *(Fig. 1)*.

3. Measure the width and length of the entire flat area to be covered. Cut out a rectangle to size. Place the pattern at each end of the rectangle and cut out the curved part *(Fig. 2)*.

Fig. 1

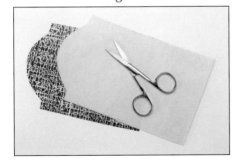

Fig. 2

SHOPPING LIST

- ☐ wood plaque
- ☐ exterior acrylic paint
- ☐ scrapbook paper
- ☐ copy paper
- ☐ pencil
- ☐ measuring tape
- ☐ matte or gloss decoupage medium
- ☐ brayer
- ☐ adhesive letters
- ☐ clear acrylic-sealer spray
- ☐ push-in picture hangers

4. Paint the plaque with a thin coat of decoupage medium, and then apply medium to the back of the paper. Set the paper in place. Smooth out any wrinkles with clean fingertips or a brayer. Let it dry. Give the plaque an additional coat of decoupage medium.

5. Cut out the letters and numbers you will need, leaving them on the backing for now. Arrange the letters on the plaque until you are happy with the way they look *(Fig. 3)*. Remove the backing from a letter positioned in the center of the plaque and apply it to the sign. Work out from the center, taking care to keep the letters aligned.

6. Finish the front and back with a coat of decoupage medium. When dry, spray the entire sign with clear acrylic-sealer spray. Attach the picture hangers to the back of the plaque.

Fig. 3

MAKE-IT-A-GIFT!

Gift a new homeowner or first-time apartment dweller with wooden numbers that mimic handmade mosaics.

Vintage or Contemporary Decorative Plates

To begin the process:

1. Remove any price tags or labels. Clean the plate to remove residue or fingerprints.

2. Place the plate on plain paper. Draw around the plate *(Fig. 1)*. With a second piece of paper, trace around the center flat part of the plate.

Fig. 1

3. Cut out a circle of scrapbook paper using the small circle template. Cut out the large circle; fold it into eighths as shown in *(Fig. 2)*.

Fig. 2

4. Open the folded circle, and then refold it in half. Sandwich three pieces of scrapbook paper between the halves. Cut out pie-shaped pieces along the fold lines. Trim away the points to fit the plate rim *(Fig. 3)*.

Fig. 3

5. Make a profile pattern by photocopying a photograph, enlarging or reducing as needed to fit the space in your plate. Carefully cut out the profile shape, then use it as a pattern to cut out the scrapbook paper.

6. Apply the profile to the center of the back of the plate with decoupage medium and allow it to dry. Next, apply the center circle to the plate. Let it dry. Finally, apply the rim pieces. When dry, give the plate a coat of medium.

7. Trace the outline of the plate on tissue paper. Cut it out slightly beyond the traced line. Cover the back of the plate with medium and the tissue circle. Smooth and pat out wrinkles and bubbles with clean fingertips. When dry, give it a final coat of medium. Use a sharp craft knife to trim any excess paper beyond the rim.

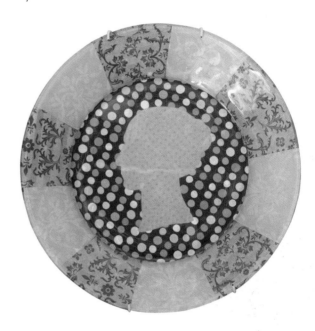

Yosemite Vacation Frame

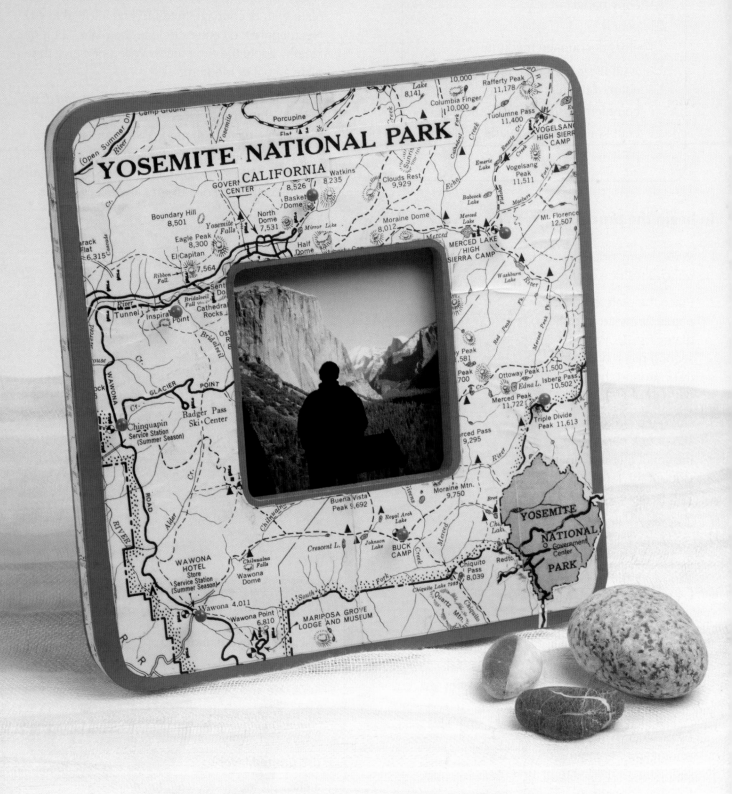

To begin the process:

1. Draw around the outer and inner edges of the frame on a piece of copy paper *(Fig. 1)*.

2. On the paper, measure and mark lines ½" inside the outer edges and ¼" inside the inner edges *(Fig. 2)*. Cut out along the marked lines. Use the pattern to cut out the shape from the vacation map.

3. With the remaining portions of the map, cut out photos or words to collage on the frame *(Fig. 3)*.

4. Paint the front and back of the frame with two or three coats of paint.

5. Apply the cut map to the frame. Smooth out wrinkles with clean fingers or a brayer. Let it dry, and then apply a coat of decoupage medium. Apply the collage pieces to the frame with medium. When dry, give the entire frame a coat of decoupage medium. Finish the frame with map pins on points of interest!

SHOPPING LIST

- ☐ unfinished wood frame, any size
- ☐ pencil
- ☐ copy paper
- ☐ measuring tape
- ☐ vacation map or map-print scrapbook paper
- ☐ acrylic paint
- ☐ matte or gloss decoupage medium
- ☐ brayer
- ☐ map pins

Fig. 3

Fig. 1

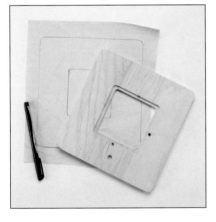

Fig. 2

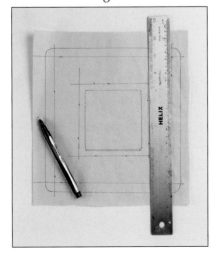

MAKE-IT-YOURS!

Already finished plain frames can always use a personal touch. Embellish them with decorative napkins or printed tissue papers. It's quick and easy.

Decorative Storage Box

Fig. 1

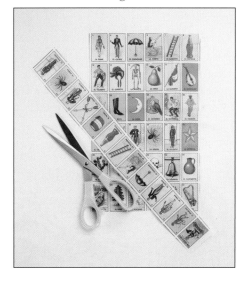

To begin the process:

1. Measure the dimensions of the box top. Cut paper to fit the top. Measure the space between the bottom of the lid and the box bottom. Cut paper strips to this width *(Fig. 1)*.

2. Apply medium to the back of a paper strip and apply it to the box, smoothing it with clean fingertips as you go. Continue adding strips to cover all four sides of the box. Let the box dry.

3. Apply medium to the top of the box and apply paper to the top. Smooth the paper as you apply it. Let it dry.

4. Cover the applied papers with a light coat of decoupage medium.

5. Spacing adhesive letters can be tricky, but this technique makes the process much easier. Cut a piece of waxed paper to the length of the line of text you need to cover the box lid. Remove each letter and place it on the waxed paper *(Fig. 2)*. Fix the letter spacing as needed, and then apply the letters to the lid. Cover the lettering with a light coat of decoupage medium.

Fig. 2

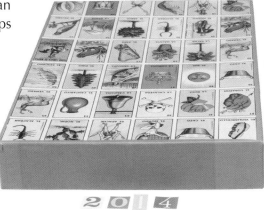

MAKE-IT-YOURS!

You won't forget what's in a storage box if you decoupage it with a reminder of what is stored inside. This set of boxes is covered with motifs cut from a novelty-print fabric.

Paper Tile Table

To begin the process:

1. Paint your object with indoor acrylic paint.

2. Measure the area you wish to tile—top, seat, or drawer fronts. Cut out a piece of wrapping paper to match your measurements. Decide on what size you want the tiles to be—the tiles pictured are about 2" square.

3. You'll want to replicate the decorative pattern of the paper. To do this, turn the wrapping paper facedown. Measure and mark the size of the tiles on the back of the paper. Starting on the right-hand side, label the first row of tiles 1, 2, 3, and so on. Label the second row 1x, 2x, and so on. Label additional rows with different letters (Fig. 1).

4. Cut apart the tiles and keep them in order.

5. Round the tile corners with a paper punch. If you lay them faceup in numerical order, left to right, you'll see the pattern (Fig. 2).

Fig. 1

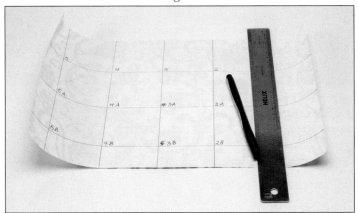

6. Lay all of the tiles in order on the surface you want to cover. Space the tiles as desired to leave a bit of "grout" between the tiles. When you're happy with the arrangement, apply each tile with decoupage medium. Smooth each tile as you go. Let the tiles dry and then apply two or more coats of decoupage medium to the tiled area.

Fig. 2

MAKE-IT-A-GIFT!

Decoupage-patterned decorative napkins on wooden hangers. Separate and remove the white napkin layers. Spray the decorative layer with two coats of clear, acrylic-sealer spray. Cut the napkin in half and then cut the napkin into short strips, keeping the strips in order. Apply the center of each strip to the front of the hanger with decoupage medium. Let the hanger dry. Then wrap and adhere each strip around the back. Give the hanger a finish coat of medium. Embellish the hanger with a ribbon bow.

To begin the process:

1. Cut your fabric into 12" to 18" sections. Spray one side of the fabric with clear acrylic sealer, let it dry, and then spray the other side *(Fig. 1)*.

Fig. 1

Fig. 2

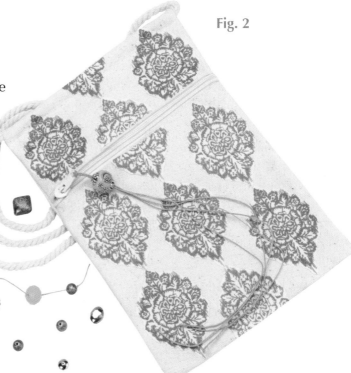

2. Cut out the pattern motifs and arrange them on the bag. You can copy the pattern of the fabric or use the motifs in your own way.

3. Use a stiff bristle brush to apply fabric decoupage medium to the back of a motif. Make sure you pay attention to the edges as you apply the medium.

4. Place the motif on the bag, and then use the brush to work medium into the fabric of the motif. Pay special attention to the edges to ensure they are well attached. Don't go beyond the edge of each motif. Let the motifs dry and then give them an additional coat of decoupage medium.

5. To make the beaded zipper pull, cut two 14" lengths of hemp beading cord and fold them in half. Thread the folded end through the pull tab, and then thread the cord ends through the folded end. Pull the cord to form a secure knot on the pull tab. Thread a large bead onto the four cords, and then thread beads onto each cord *(Fig. 2)*. Finish each cord with an overhand knot and trim the cord ends.

MAKE-IT-A-GIFT!

Decoupage bright and cheerful fabric motifs to an inexpensive pair of canvas shoes.

Shades of India
Purse

Decoupaged Jewelry

To begin the process:

1. Paint the edges of the bare wood shapes *(Fig. 1)*.

2. Draw around the shapes on copy paper to make a pattern for the scrapbook paper. Cut two pieces per shape. Use decoupage medium to apply the papers to the shapes one side at a time. Let them dry. Trim any overhanging paper edges with a craft knife.

Fig. 1

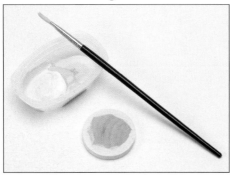

3. Give the shapes a finish coat of decoupage medium on each side.

4. To add beads to the edges, mark the bead spacing with a pencil. Then use an awl or sharp tapestry needle to pierce the marked spots. (Hold a tapestry needle with flat-nose pliers.)

5. Thread one or two beads onto the headpins and one eye pin. Use wire cutters to shorten the length of the pins, leaving about ¼" below the beads. Fit each pin into a pierced spot and trim it so the bead fits flush against the edge *(Fig. 2)*.

Fig. 2

SHOPPING LIST

- ☐ craft wood shapes
- ☐ pencil
- ☐ copy paper
- ☐ scrapbook paper
- ☐ gloss or matte decoupage medium
- ☐ craft knife
- ☐ awl or sharp tapestry needle
- ☐ wire cutters
- ☐ 2 pairs of flat-nose pliers
- ☐ assorted small beads
- ☐ acrylic paint
- ☐ head pins, eye pins, ear wires, chain, and clasp
- ☐ two-part epoxy or beading glue

6. Use a headpin to push some glue into each spot and to place a drop of glue on the end of each beaded pin. Put the pins in place. Use another headpin to wipe off any excess glue. Let the glue dry overnight before you attach any chains or ear wires.

7. Use two pairs of jewelry pliers to open and close the eye pins, jump rings, and ear wires—the technique is the same for all of them. Hold a jump ring with pliers on either side of the cut wire. Push one end forward and the other in the opposite direction. Close it in the same way. Attach ear wires to head pins, clasp to the chain, and pendants to the chain using this simple technique. See sidebar on page 32 for information about basic jewelry tools.

EARRING VARIATIONS

The same techniques can be used to make earrings in multiple styles— indulge your imagination!

MUST-HAVE JEWELRY TOOLS!

There are four basic jewelry tools that should be in every crafter's tool kit: flat-nose pliers, round-nose pliers, wire cutters, and a pair of chain-nose pliers.

Flat-nose pliers should have smooth inner surfaces. They're versatile tools for holding and bending sharp angles.

Round-nose pliers are used to form loops and make curved bends in wire. With practice, you can even learn to make your own ear wires and simple clasps.

Chain-nose pliers are used with flat-nose pliers for opening and closing jump rings, shortening chains, and attaching clasps and ear wires. Use them with your flat-nose pliers to do those jobs.

Wire cutters should be used only to cut thin jewelry wire. Don't try to cut thick, steel wire with them or you'll ruin them.

Mod Podge® is a registered trademark of Plaid Enterprises, Inc., Norcross, Georgia, USA